Sabine Lohf

CHRISTMAS CRAFTS

Sabine Lohf

CHRISTMAS CRAFTS

A Christmas craft
book for children
4 years and up

CP CHILDRENS PRESS®
CHICAGO

Translation by Mrs. Werner Lippmann and Mrs. Ruth Bookey

Library of Congress Cataloging-in-Publication Data

Lohf, Sabine.
    [Himmelsleiter und so weiter.   English]
    Christmas crafts / by Sabine Lohf.
        p.   cm.
    Translation of: Himmelsleiter und so weiter.
    Summary: Instructions for making Christmas craft projects, gifts,
and decorations.
    ISBN 0-516-09252-9
    1. Christmas decorations—Juvenile literature.   2. Handicraft—
Juvenile literature.   I. Title.
    [DNLM: 1. Christmas decorations.   2. Handicraft.]
TT900.C4L6413   1989
745.594'12—dc20   89-22255
                                                                              CIP
                                                                              AC

Published in the United States in 1990 by Childrens Press®, Inc.,
5440 North Cumberland Avenue, Chicago, IL 60656.

Contents

Decorated Matchboxes

You will need:

24 empty matchboxes, glue, colored construction paper, feathers, scissors, needle and thread

Decide which color paper you want to use and arrange the matchboxes on it in a pattern you like. If you wish, you can copy the pattern in the large picture on the right.

Example:

a) Glue a matchbox onto the colored paper.

b) Cut out a duck (or swan) head.

c) Bend a small piece at the bottom so that you can glue it onto the box.

Bend here and glue on box.

If you would like to hang the box: Slide out the inside of the matchbox and make a hanger in the middle part of the outer box with the needle and thread.

If you want to hang the box sideways, put the thread through here.

Don't tell what is in the box!

Put a surprise in every box.
Each box is hung on a string. ✱

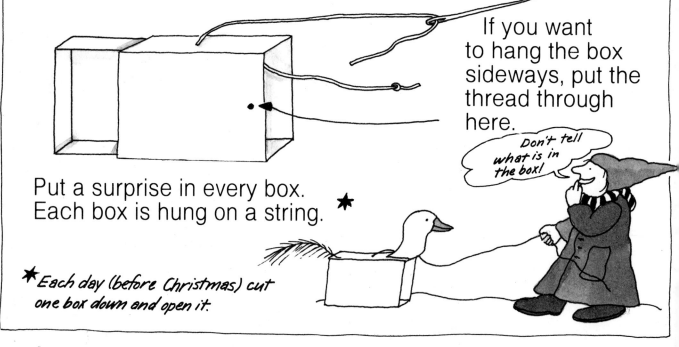

✱ *Each day (before Christmas) cut one box down and open it.*

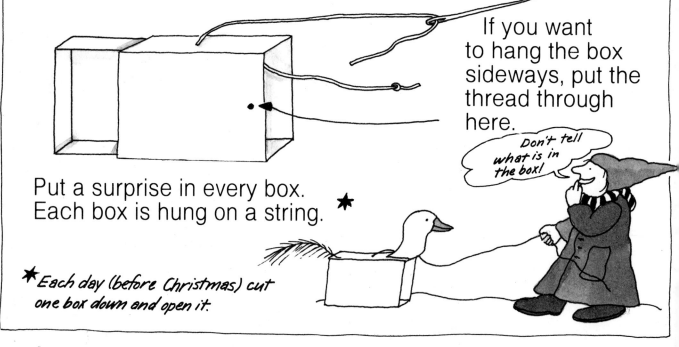

A surprise in every box

Papier-Mâché Goose

You will need:

Newspapers, papier-mâché paste, 1 balloon, glue, a plastic bowl, white and yellow paint, brushes, scissors, a few white feathers, many little boxes, wrapping paper and ribbons

1. Mix the papier-mâché paste with water in the plastic bowl. (There will be instructions on the package.)

2. Blow up the balloon and tie it so that no air can escape.

3. Tear newspapers into strips. Brush the strips thickly with paste. Wrap strip after strip around the balloon until you have 4 or 5 layers.

4. Shape the head and neck from paper strips that are soaked with paste. Attach the neck to the balloon with more paper strips. Let everything dry overnight.

5. Glue tail feathers on the back.

6. When the goose is dry, cut a hole in the top of the body and paint the goose.

Later it will be ready to fill with the surprise packages wrapped in paper and ribbons.

No!

Now I'll paint you.

**Stuffed
Christmas goose**

A Castle Made Out of Boxes

You will need:

Different-sized boxes, cardboard tubes from toilet-paper and paper-towel rolls, aluminum foil, shiny paper, 2 Christmas-tree balls, glue, a heavy piece of cardboard (as a base for the castle), a sharp knife, silver spray paint

1. Glue all the boxes onto the heavy cardboard to build the castle. Make sure that the boxes are opened.

2. Cut doors and windows with the knife where you can't open the boxes. (CAUTION: Be careful when using a knife, or have an adult do the cutting for you.)

3. When you've completed steps 1 & 2, spray the castle on all sides with the silver paint. Glue on the balls.

4. While the castle is drying, cut out some steeples for the towers from the foil.

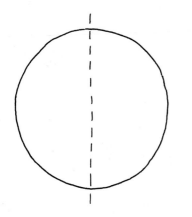

Cut out a large circle, then cut the circle into halves. Roll each half circle into a steeple shape (like a pointed hat).

Glue the steeples to the top of the cardboard tubes to make the towers of your castle.

Finally, glue some of the shiny paper on your castle. Leave it in your room overnight and maybe you will find some little surprises in the castle in the morning.

The castle has many secrets

A Big Red Truck

<u>You will need:</u>

Heavy cardboard, one large and one small box, another large open box for the back of the truck, two wooden sticks, glue, paints, scissors, some heavy white paper

1. Cut the heavy cardboard so that the two large boxes can fit exactly on it. Glue them on the cardboard as shown.

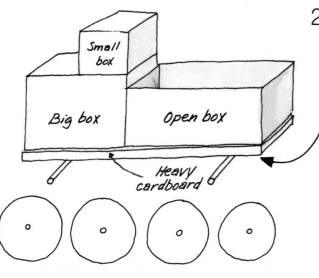

2. Glue the sticks under the cardboard.

3. Cut 4 circles out of cardboard.

4. Cut a hole into the center of each circle, so that when you put the circles on the sticks, they will turn like wheels. Then cut out four smaller circles and glue them onto the ends of the sticks to keep the wheels on. Let the glue dry.

5. Paint the truck. Paint or draw a driver (Santa's helper) for the truck and glue it to the side of the cab.

6. Now fill the truck with little gifts.

Christmas mail

Angel Choir

You can use the angel choir as an advent calendar.

You will need:

24 cardboard tubes from toilet-paper rolls, white crepe paper, heavy white paper, pink paper, white "Easter" grass, scissors, tape, ribbons, waxed paper, felt-tip markers, glue

1. Cut the pink paper into strips wide enough to use as a face when glued onto the top of the toilet-paper tube.

2. For the dress, cut the white crepe paper to fit around the lower part of the tube. Fasten the dress with tape in the back of the tube. Tie a pretty ribbon around the middle of the dress as a belt.

3. Cut arms out of the white paper and glue one on each side of the tube. Use pink paper for the hands and glue them on the ends of the arms.

4. Paint a face on your angel.

Make wings out of waxed paper and glue on.

Glue circle here.

You can hide a little gift inside the angel by gluing a circle onto the bottom of the tube.

You can make hair for the angel with excelsior, white "Easter" grass, or yarn. Stick the hair into the open top of the angel. Invite friends to help you.

There will be
surprises tomorrow

Sky Ladder

You will need:

2 same-sized cardboard box covers; white and grey cardboard for clouds, ladder, and house; scissors; glue; cotton batting; paints and paintbrush

Cut the clouds out of the white cardboard and glue on the cotton.

Back wall

Glue here.

Floor

Glue two box covers together.

The ladder will be made out of two long cardboard strips with 23 smaller strips glued across them for the steps.

Paint the house.

Cut this shape out of cardboard.

The dotted lines show where to bend and glue the ends together.

Cut a roof for your house.

Cut a door into the house.

24

The 24th surprise will be hidden in the house.

Hang 23 little surprises, one on each ladder rung.

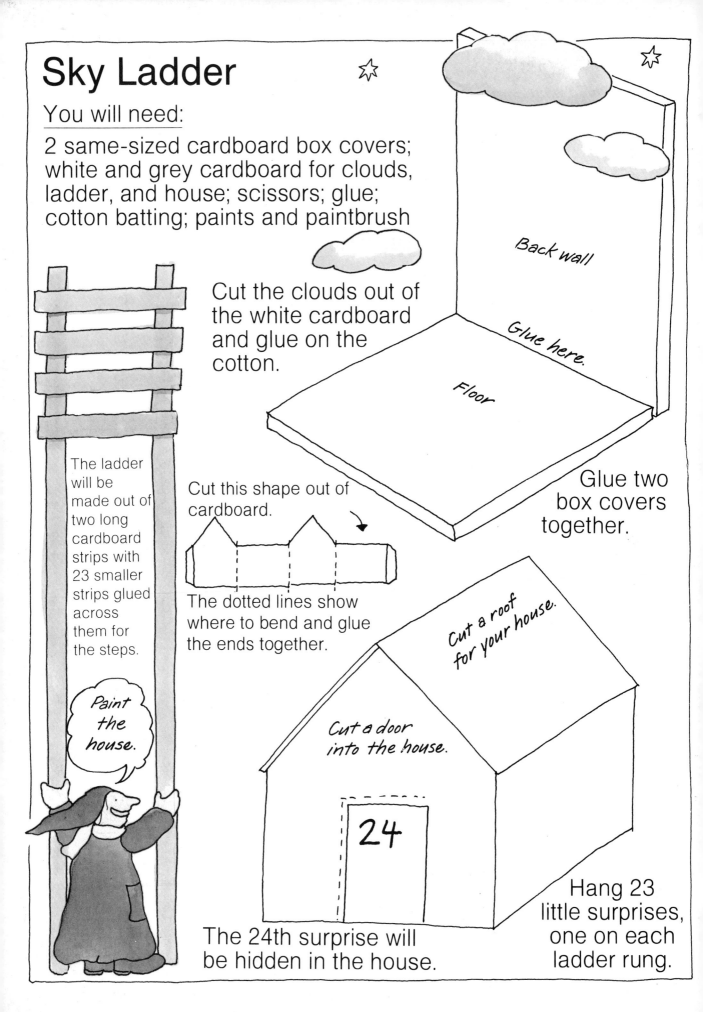

Ladder to the sky

Sun Advent Calendar

You will need:

1 large sheet of yellow poster board, 1 small sheet of orange poster board, yellow construction paper, crayons, glue, 1 brass paper fastener, scissors, paper clips

1. Cut a large yellow circle from the poster board.

2. Cut 25 sunrays from the yellow construction paper. Glue them around the edge of the sun. Do the gluing on the back of the sun.

3. Paint a face on the sun.

4. Cut out a "pointer" from the small poster board and fasten it to the sun with the paper fastener.

Turn the pointer one number each day.

I wish I had a dog.

Let's go to the zoo.

I wish

Write wishes or draw little pictures on each of the sunrays.

5. Roll up each ray and hold it closed with a paper clip.

6. Number the rolled rays 1 through 25. Hang up the sun. Each day, starting with December 1st, unroll a sunray and look at the picture or wish on it. When the 25th is unrolled, it will be Christmas!

**Sun
with
wishing rays**

Angel Marionette

You will need:

1 large plastic foam ball for a head, 1 box of cotton batting, white cloth and other cloth scraps, scissors, needle and thread, felt-tip markers, a cardboard toilet-paper tube, some wire, old curtain material or plastic wrap, "angel hair," some string

1. Fold the white cloth in half. Cut out the body, arms, and legs (see drawing). Sew the body, arms, and legs where you see the dotted lines.

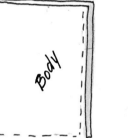

Maybe someone can sew all these parts on a sewing machine for you.
★ ★

2. Glue the foam ball on the toilet-paper tube. Paint a face on the ball.

3. Stuff the body with the cotton. Put the toilet-paper tube into the body and tie the string around the neck to secure it to the body. Sew on the arms and legs. Sew a dress for the angel, and dress her. Bend the wire into a wing shape. Cover the shape with the curtain material or plastic wrap and sew it to the angel's back.

Glue hair on head.

Sew wings to back.

Attach long strings to the top of the head and to the hands so that you will be able to make the angel walk and dance.

"I bring
you tidings of
great joy"

Milk-Carton Lamp

You can also hang these lanterns on a stick for your porch or patio.

You will need:

Empty milk cartons, white spray paint, knife, glue, colored transparent paper, white drawing paper, a small flashlight

Cut a hole.

1. Wash out an empty milk carton and let it dry.

2. Cut windows and doors into the milk carton with the knife. (CAUTION: Be careful when using a knife, or have an adult do the cutting for you.)

3. Make a door large enough to fit your hand through at the back of the milk carton.

4. Spray-paint the "house" white.

5. Let the paint dry and glue the colored transparent paper over the windows and doors. Do this from the inside, reaching through the door you cut in the back. It is easiest if you cover the windows and door with one piece of the transparent paper.

6. Cut a hole in the "roof," and make a chimney by rolling a piece of the white paper and inserting it in the hole you cut in the roof. Light the small flashlight and place it inside your lamp.

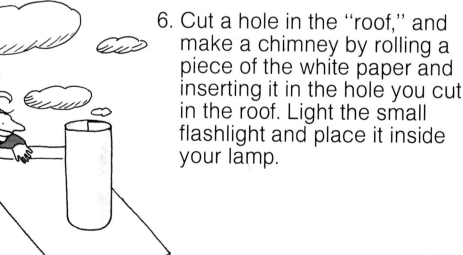

Hurray! It works.

Milk-carton
city
with lights

Bird Lantern

You will need:

2 balloons, colored tissue paper, papier-mâché paste, a brush, string, glue, scissors, a stick, a small flashlight

1. Mix the papier-mâché paste, following the directions on the package.

2. Blow up the balloons. Make one larger than the other.

3. Brush the tissue paper with the paste mixture and stick the paper over each balloon until they are thoroughly covered. Let everything dry for two days.

4. Cut a hole in the top of the large balloon and one on the side of the small balloon.

Glue a beak on the small balloon.

If you want to light up the head too, cut out two eyes near the top of the head.

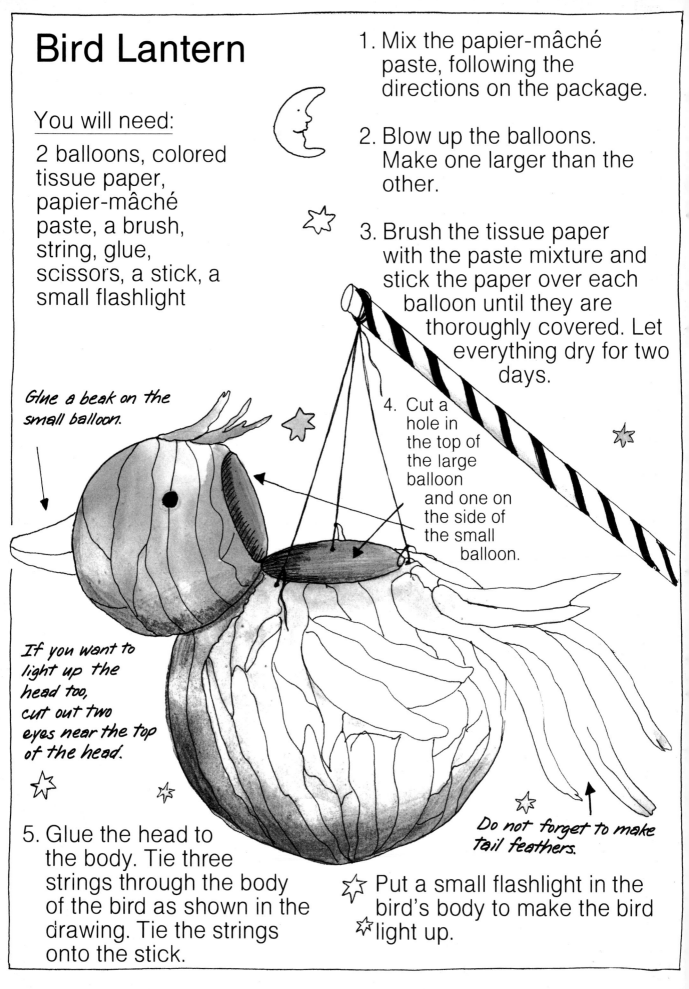

Do not forget to make tail feathers.

5. Glue the head to the body. Tie three strings through the body of the bird as shown in the drawing. Tie the strings onto the stick.

☆ Put a small flashlight in the bird's body to make the bird light up.

The
bright
bird

Aluminum-Foil Swans

You will need:

1 roll of aluminum foil, a white cardboard carton, scissors, a wide bowl, votive candles

Cut off a large sheet of foil and crush it into a loose ball.

Squeeze the center section of the foil into a round belly shape. Shape one end of the foil into the neck and head and the other end into a tail.

Flatten the bottom of the body on a flat surface so that the swan can sit on its belly. Make sure it is balanced so that it can float in water.

Fill a bowl with water, float your swans and some votive candles. The light from the candles will make the aluminum-foil swans sparkle. (CAUTION: Have an adult light the candles for you. Do not leave the room while the candles are burning.)

Create a winter scene by putting some houses made from the white box around your pond.

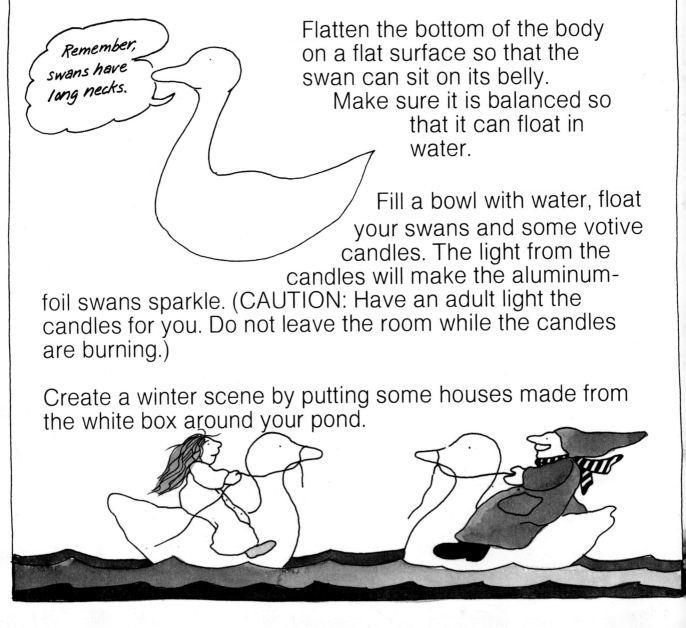

Silver lake
at night

Folded Jumping Jacks

You will need:

Gold foil, white tracing paper, crepe paper, scissors, small white plastic foam balls, pins with red heads, needle and thread, glue

Cut up to here.

Cut 2 equal-length strips of gold foil and fold them back and forth over each other until you get to the cut ends. Then fold each leg the way you did the body.

Fold arms from strips of foil and glue them to the top of the body.

Cut a half circle from the foil to make a pointed hat.

Make a nose with a red-tipped pen.

With the needle and thread, sew through the top of the body, then through a foam ball, and finally through the hat. (See the drawing.)

Cut and sew some white crepe paper to make a collar for each jumping jack.

For the angel, fold a piece of gold foil and use tracing paper for the wings.

**Light
and easy**

Three Kings

You will need:

3 empty plastic bottles, newspapers, papier-mâché paste, paint brush, wire, crepe paper, cloth scraps, yarn, scissors, clear tape, sand

1. Put sand into the bottle so that it doesn't tip over.

2. Crumple newspapers into a ball and stick the ball on top of the bottle. Fasten with tape.

3. Mix the papier-mâché paste as directed on the package.

4. Wrap a long piece of wire around the bottle neck several times and extend this wire to make arms.

5. Wrap newspaper several times around the arms. Fasten with tape.

6. Tear newspaper into long, narrow strips. Cover the strips thickly with paste and wrap them around the head and arms.

7. Make three of these figures. Put them in a warm place until they are good and dry. Then paint the heads.

8. Wrap the bottles and the arms with crepe paper and tape it on.

9. The three kings need crowns, yarn hair, and some clothes and capes made from cloth scraps. Make them some belts and jewelry. If you want the kings to carry candles as in the picture, have an adult help you. Put the kings outside before the candles are lit.

**Three
wise men**

Hand Puppets

You will need:

1 bag plaster of paris, 1 bowl, water, 2 wooden sticks, 2 empty bottles, newspapers, paints, red and white felt, cloth scraps, needle, thread, scissors, glue

1. Mix the plaster of paris in the bowl, following the directions on the package.

2. Put a wooden stick into the bottle. Put crushed newspaper on top of the stick. The paper must be above the bottle neck.

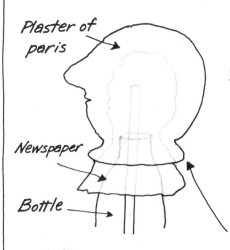

Plaster of paris

Newspaper

Bottle

3. Shape a head over the newspaper. Keep smoothing it out, again and again, with plaster and water. The neck should be wider at the bottom.

4. The heads should dry for two to three days before you paint them.

5. To make clothes, sew two felt pieces together at the top and sides.

Cut off.

Cut off.

The hands are cut out of some cloth and stuck to the sleeves.

A girl doll gets yarn hair and a Santa Claus gets a red hat.

Pull the dress over the neck and tie tightly.

Play with us

Weaving With Paper

You will need:

Aluminum foil and colored foil, pretty wrapping paper, ribbons, scissors, glue

1. Put a large rectangular piece of foil on the table and cut along the lines shown in the drawing.

2. Tear or cut the wrapping paper into strips for weaving, and pull the strips through the cut areas.

3. Then fasten the paper strips with glue at the edges to secure them.

Row 2

Row 1

4. Weave with different-colored strips until the whole piece is covered.

5. Now you can use it as a place mat or give it as a present.

It glitters and crackles

Candy Jumping Jacks

You will need:

A plastic foam wreath, crepe paper in all colors, paste, scissors, construction paper, pins, thread, lots of candies

1. This is the way you make the jumping jack:

   Tie five candies together with thread. (See the drawing.)

2. Cut a face and a cap out of colored paper and stick them to the top of the candyman.

3. Then cut 2-inch strips from crepe paper and wind these around the foam wreath.

4. Hang the candymen on the wreath, and if you like, hang more candies on it.

Candy wreath

Gingerbread Village

<u>You will need:</u>

Stiff gingerbread, white-dotted chocolate candy, thick cardboard, 1 wooden board, 1 knife, 1 paint brush. For the sugar icing, you will need a bowl, 2 or 3 egg whites, and powdered sugar. Use anything you like for the decorations.

1. Cut the gingerbread into thick slices on the wooden board. (CAUTION: Be careful when using a knife, or have an adult do the cutting for you.)

2. Put the egg whites and powdered sugar in the bowl and mix until thick.

3. Take the heavy cardboard and use a large paintbrush to put sugar icing on the place where the first house will stand.

To make the little houses:

Use two thick slices of gingerbread for the side walls. Use sugar icing for "mortar" between all the pieces. Cut two half slices for the front and back walls. Cut two more slices to fit for the roof. Make two three-cornered pieces to fit for the gable ends. Fill in the gap at the top of the roof with a small rectangular piece. Make a square chimney. Dribble sugar icing "snow" on the roof and walls.

All the little houses are built in this way. They can be as big or as small as you wish. When the village is assembled, the rest of the cardboard base can be covered with more icing and the chocolate candies. Sprinkle powdered sugar over everything for extra snow.

Gingerbread houses

A Christmas Candy Stand

You will need:

A big box, colored construction paper, several insides of matchboxes, string, clothespins, all kinds of candies, a cardboard toilet-paper tube for the man, cotton batting, strips of felt, scissors, tape, glue

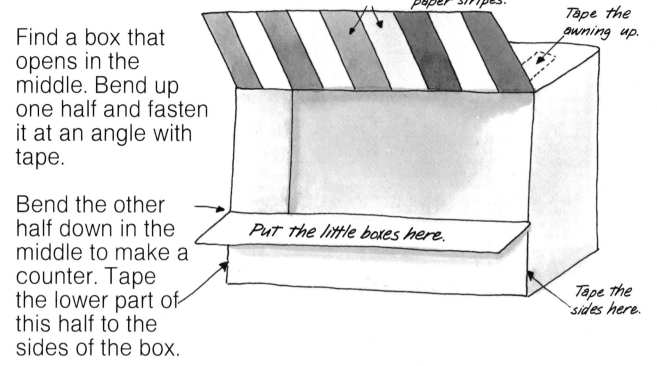

Make some construction-paper stripes.

Tape the awning up.

Find a box that opens in the middle. Bend up one half and fasten it at an angle with tape.

Bend the other half down in the middle to make a counter. Tape the lower part of this half to the sides of the box.

Put the little boxes here.

Tape the sides here.

For the salesman, wrap the cardboard tube with colored paper. Make a head of cotton batting and give him a paper cap. The arms are rolled from construction paper and glued to the body.

Glue on the cap.

Glue on the arms.

Now fill all the boxes with candies for sale. You can also hang up things with a string and the clothespins. You could put little boxes and jars in front of the stand.

Christmas candy stand

Decorated Branch

You will need:

A pretty dried branch, beads, feathers, white and colored paper, glue, scissors, needle and thread, an empty bottle to stick the branch into

To make snowflakes:

1. Fold a square piece of paper in the middle.

2. Fold once again in the middle.

3. Then cut on the indicated line.

A

Fold here

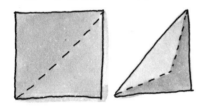

B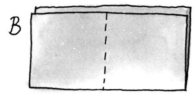

C

If you want the star to have more points, you must fold the paper shown at C above once more diagonally. Then cut on the indicated line.

You can cut patterns on all the outside edges. Unfold the paper carefully and you have a snowflake!

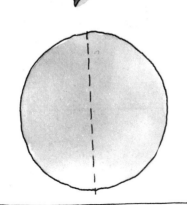

To make cones:

Cut out a circle, fold it in the middle, and roll the half circle into a cone. Glue the edges together, pull a thread through, and hang the little cones on your branch tree.

A Christmas branch for you

Cheerful Gift Wrapping

You will need:

An empty can with a cover, a cardboard tube from a toilet-paper roll, gray cardboard, some gray construction paper (also other colors), small boxes, some string, scissors, glue

1. Cut the gray paper to fit exactly around the can and glue it on. This will be a donkey.

This can will be a donkey.

2. Cut the head from gray paper. Roll it and glue it together. Stuff pink paper into the bottom for the mouth.

3. Cut two ears of gray paper and glue them to the head.

4. The legs are cut from the gray cardboard and glued to the can.

5. Stuff the donkey full of little presents and put the lid on the can. The donkey can also carry little packages on his back.

The Santa Claus is made like the angels on page 14. But Santa gets a hat instead of hair. Before the hat is tied off on top with string, put a little surprise package inside. The donkey and the Santa Claus will be welcome surprise gifts.

Donkey with a special delivery

Nutty Characters

You will need:

One package of clay of different colors, walnuts, hazelnuts, crepe paper, glue, scissors, 4 buttons, 2 matchsticks, felt-tip markers

Nut People

Make feet out of clay. Put a walnut on the feet for the lower body. (You might have to glue the walnut.) Shape the upper body out of clay and press it onto the nut. Make clay arms and attach them to the upper body.
On top of the upper body, glue another walnut for the head.

Draw the face with a felt-tip marker.

Cut out little crepe-paper hats and noses and glue them on the heads of your nut people.

If the nut people won't stand up, glue them to cardboard.

A Nut-Baby in a Buggy

Glue a hazlenut on the back of half a walnut shell. Glue two matchsticks under the walnut shell. On each end of the sticks, glue a button. Give the baby a face and a hat.

You can make nut bugs from half a walnut shell and a hazelnut.

Half walnut shell

Clay

Hazelnut

Can you think of ways to make other nut animals?

**Nut people
have a party**

Peanut and Potato People

<u>You will need:</u>

Peanuts, potatoes, matchsticks, crepe paper, gold paper, thin gold-colored string, pins with glass heads, clay, glue

Use straight pins with glass heads for eyes.

Put some glue here.

Put a pin through here for extra holding power.

1. Look for a potato that has a hump like a camel. You will need two long peanuts, one for the neck and one for the head.

2. Glue the peanuts to the potato, push four matchsticks into the potato for legs, and you have a camel! Use gold string to tie packs on the camels.

Stick a pin through here.

Use a toothpick for a walking stick.

Make crowns of gold paper for the kings and glue them on.

Make a cape or coat from crepe paper.

The kings are each made of one long and one round peanut. Glue them together and glue two matchsticks onto the long peanut for arms and two for legs. Push the legs into a piece of clay so that the figures can stand.

Peanut King's caravan

Citrus People

You will need:

Oranges, grapefruit, lemons, cloves, cinnamon sticks, construction paper, glue, toothpicks, tissue paper, peanuts, needle and thread

After you squeeze the juice from grapefruit, oranges, and lemons, save the skins. Scrape the pulp from the inside and let the skins dry out on newspaper.

Then you can make people and a turtle. Make construction-paper hats for your people. What other figures can you make?

Attach cinnamon-stick arms with pins.

The eyes are cloves.

Paste on a paper mouth.

Fold a rectangular piece of tissue paper.
Sew through the top of the folded paper. Pull the thread tight. Make three of these and fasten them on a stick. Now you have a parasol.

The turtle has a peanut head and legs.

The citrus family out for a walk

Christmas-Tree Birds

You will need:

Gold paper, felt-tip marker, feathers, scissors, sequins, Christmas-tree balls, glue, thread, tissue paper

Ball bird:

1. Cut a bird's head, feet, and tail feathers from gold paper. Glue them to the Christmas-tree ball.

Let's find the Christmas tree.

Bird with folding wings:

2. Cut a bird body out of cardboard. Cut a slit in the middle of the body.

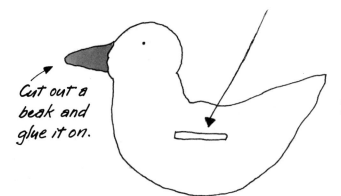

Cut out a beak and glue it on.

3. Make accordion folds in a sheet of tissue paper. Push the folded tissue paper through the slit in the bird's body.

Sequin bird:

4. Cut a bird shape out of cardboard. Cover it with glue and press different-colored sequins into the glue. *Glue on a feather for the bird's tail.*

A flock of birds

Incense-Holder Figures

<u>You will need:</u>

Clay, a plastic sheet, a little bowl of water, 1 nail with a big head, a teaspoon

1. Cover the table with the plastic sheet. Break off a chunk of clay. Knead it with the flat of your hand to remove air bubbles.

2. Shape the clay into a roll. Put a ball on top for the head. (See the drawing.)

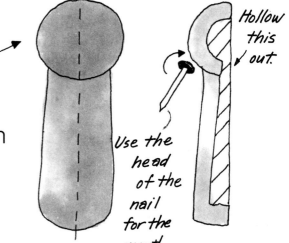

Hollow this out.

Use the head of the nail for the mouth.

3. Cut this form in half down through the middle. Hollow out the halves with a spoon. A thin wall (¼ inch) must remain all around.

4. Take a piece of clay and put it into a bowl of water. Spread this soft and slippery clay ("slip"), on the edges of the two hollowed-out halves and put them together again. Make a hole about 1 inch in diameter in the top of the head. The incense will go in here. Poke holes for the eyes and mouth through the clay of the head. Make sure the holes go all the way through. Pinch the clay to form a nose.

5. Then put slip over the area where the two halves are joined and smooth out the seams.

6. Use the slip to attach arms made of rolled clay. Make little clay hats for the figures. Poke a row of holes all the way through the hats around the crown. Let the figures dry on newspaper for two weeks; then have them fired in a kiln.

7. Put some incense into the figure through the hole in the head. Have an adult light the incense for you. Then replace the hat.

Incense-holder figures

Dancing Paper Snake

You will need:

Thin colorful paper for the snake, some heavy paper, scissors, glue, felt-tip markers, a few little stars, cotton batting, needle and thread

1. Cut a circle from thin colorful paper.

2. Draw a spiral on the paper and cut on the lines of the spiral.

Stick some stars on the snake.

Make hair from cotton.

3. Draw a dancing person on heavy paper and cut it out.

4. Leave an extra piece of paper on the bottom of one foot when you cut out the person.

Bend tab back.

5. Bend the tab on the bottom of the foot and glue it to the head of the paper snake.

6. Color the person on both sides or glue colorful paper on it.

7. Hang the figure over a radiator. The heat from the radiator will make the snake dance.

**Everything turns
and whirls**

Walnut Ducks on a Wreath

You will need:

Walnuts, a nutcracker, white paper, feathers, white thread, gold spray paint, a plastic foam wreath, a yellow felt-tip marker, a straight pin, gold crepe paper, scissors, glue, newspapers

1. Cut a long, wide strip of crepe paper and wind it around the wreath.

Attach start of paper strip to wreath with a pin.

2. Crack a few walnuts carefully; the halves should not be broken. Take out the nut meats.

3. Put the walnut shells on newspaper and spray them with gold paint.

4. Cut duck heads out of white paper. Cut a slit into the neck to fit on the walnut half. (See the drawing.)

5. Tie threads around the nuts and knot them.

6. Color the beak with the felt-tip marker and stick a feather on the back.

7. Hang all the ducks on the wreath.

Golden ducks

Shoe-Box Theater

You will need:

A large shoe or boot box, heavy paper, colored construction paper, glue, scissors, sharp knife (CAUTION: Be careful with the knife, or have an adult do the cutting for you.)

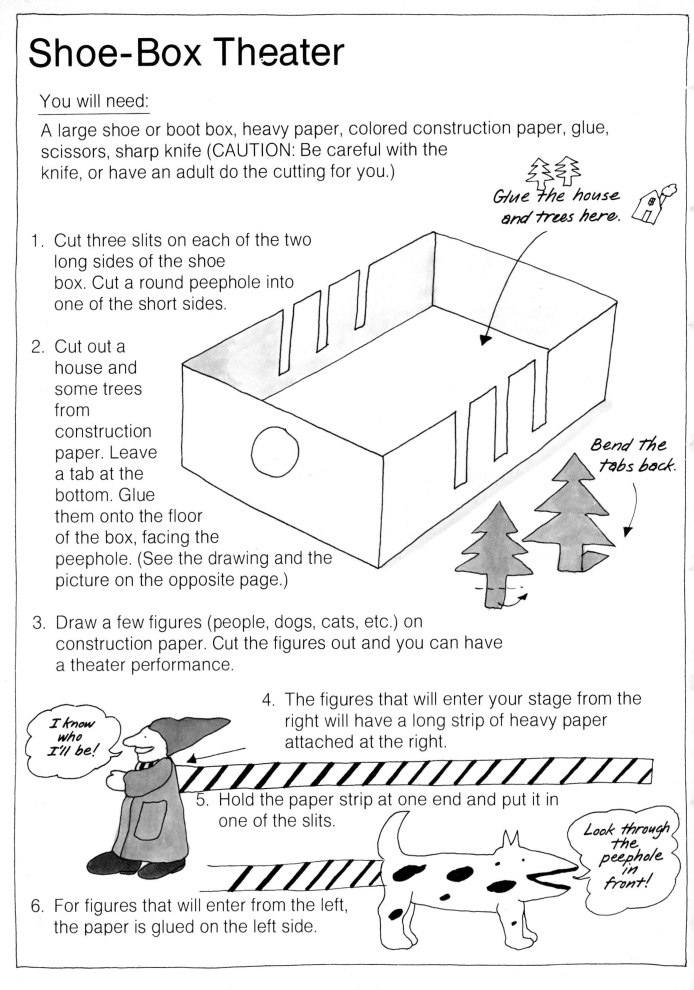

Glue the house and trees here.

1. Cut three slits on each of the two long sides of the shoe box. Cut a round peephole into one of the short sides.

2. Cut out a house and some trees from construction paper. Leave a tab at the bottom. Glue them onto the floor of the box, facing the peephole. (See the drawing and the picture on the opposite page.)

Bend the tabs back.

3. Draw a few figures (people, dogs, cats, etc.) on construction paper. Cut the figures out and you can have a theater performance.

4. The figures that will enter your stage from the right will have a long strip of heavy paper attached at the right.

I know who I'll be!

5. Hold the paper strip at one end and put it in one of the slits.

Look through the peephole in front!

6. For figures that will enter from the left, the paper is glued on the left side.

Here comes
Santa Claus

Nativity Scene

You will need:

Clay in different colors, sturdy paper, crepe paper, foil, needle and thread, scissors, glue, yarn, cotton batting, small paper rolls

Form clay heads for:

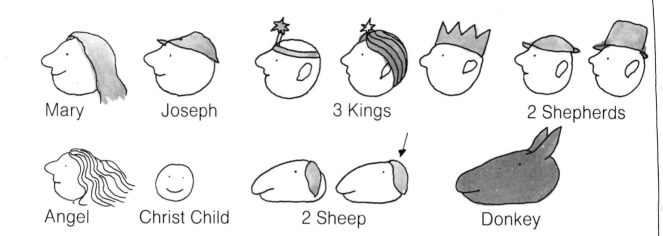

Mary   Joseph   3 Kings   2 Shepherds

Angel   Christ Child   2 Sheep   Donkey

Glue the heads onto small rolls that you have made from heavy paper.

The arms are made the same way, but make the paper rolls smaller. Make crowns for the kings with foil or gold paper. Make paper hats for the shepherds and Joseph. Cut paper ears for the sheep. Make a crepe-paper veil for Mary. Put yarn hair on the angel.

Make crepe-paper capes: Pull a thread through the top of a square of crepe paper and tie the cape under the head of a figure.
(See the drawing.)

Glue the figures onto cardboard.

Glue cotton "wool" on the sheep.

Bethlehem
manger

INDEX